french desserts

french desserts

Laura Washburn

photography by Martin Brigdale

RYLAND
PETERS
& SMALL

LONDON NEW YORK

First published in the USA in 2005
by Ryland Peters & Small, Inc.
519 Broadway, 5th Floor
New York, NY 10012
www.rylandpeters.com

10 9 8 7 6 5 4 3 2 1

Library of Congress
Cataloging-in-Publication Data

Washburn, Laura.
  French desserts / Laura Washburn ;
photography by Martin Brigdale.
    p. cm.
  Includes index.
  ISBN 1-84172-958-2
  1. Desserts. 2. Cookery, French. I.
Title.
  TX773.W335 2005
  641.8'6'0944--dc22
                        2005005601

Acknowledgments
Mille fois merci to all at Ryland Peters &
Small. Thank you Martin Brigdale for yet
more beautiful photographs, Bridget
Sargeson for perfect presentation, and
Helen Trent for impeccable taste. For
everyone else—the list is too long to cite
here but you know who you are—thanks.
And wink wink for Jules and Clara.

Senior Designer Steve Painter
Commissioning Editor
     Elsa Petersen-Schepelern
Editor Susan Stuck
Production Patricia Harrington
Art Director Gabriella Le Grazie
Publishing Director Alison Starling

Food Stylist Bridget Sargeson
Prop Stylist Helen Trent

Notes
• All spoon measurements are
level unless otherwise specified.
• All eggs are extra-large unless
otherwise specified. Uncooked
or partially cooked eggs should
not be served to the very young,
the very old, those with
compromised immune systems,
or to pregnant women.

• Before baking, measure all
ingredients exactly and prepare
baking sheets or pans.
• Ovens should be preheated to
the specified temperature. Recipes
in this book were tested in several
kinds of oven—all work slightly
differently. I recommend using
an oven thermometer and
consulting the maker's handbook
for special instructions.

contents

introduction

From mousses to tarts, ices to pastries, France has provided us with some of our favorite sweet things. There is a great tradition of pastry making in France and one of the things that struck me when I first went there was the window displays in all the pastry shops. Forget the museums—there was always going to be something beautiful to look at in the pâtisserie, no matter how tiny the village.

But it wasn't always that way. Sweet and savory baking traditionally went hand in hand, but this caused disputes between bakers and butchers as to who had more right to sell certain goods. So pastry shops evolved as a way to resolve the problem, and all things sweet went the way of the pâtisserie. The distinction seems to have blurred again, as boulangeries and pâtisseries all sell a bit of both, but the giveaway is always in the presentation: rows and rows of neatly arranged and mouth-wateringly attractive desserts that tempt the eye as much as the palate.

This perhaps makes it sound as if preparing French desserts at home is going to be a challenge, but all of the recipes in this book have been adapted for the home cook. They are all straightforward, require no specialized skills and taste as good as they look.

For people who enjoy cooking, it is never really a chore to prepare a meal, and there is something especially satisfying about making dessert. It is certainly the part that is most appreciated. And you don't even need a meal as an excuse, because any occasion and any time of day is always a good reason.

Traditionally, Napoléons (also called *millefeuilles* or "thousand leaves") are rectangles of puff pastry alternating with layers of pastry cream, topped with marbled fondant icing. This recipe is a departure from tradition, with a more interesting combination of flavors (and is much prettier too).

napoléons with lemon cream and strawberries
napoléons au citron et aux fraises

1 lb. package of puff pastry

milk (see method)

sugar (see method)

1¾ lb. strawberries, thinly sliced

confectioners' sugar, to serve

lemon cream

2 extra-large whole eggs and 3 egg yolks

⅓ cup sugar

freshly squeezed juice of 3 lemons, strained

6 tablespoons unsalted butter, cut into pieces

½ cup heavy cream, chilled

a baking sheet, lined with parchment paper

serves 4–5

Roll out the dough to a large square just under ½ inch thick. Cut out rectangles about 5 x 3 inches. You should get about 10 rectangles.

Arrange the rectangles on the lined baking sheet. Brush with milk and sprinkle with sugar. Bake in a preheated oven at 400°F until puffed and golden, 10–15 minutes. Remove. When cool, carefully cut each one in half horizontally, using a serrated knife, to obtain 2 thin layers.

To make the lemon cream, mix the eggs, egg yolks, and sugar in a saucepan. Add the lemon juice and whisk lightly. Add the pieces of butter and cook over low heat, stirring constantly until thick. Remove from the heat, transfer to a bowl, and let cool. (The recipe can be made up to 1 day in advance up to this point.)

No more than a few hours before serving, whip the cream until it holds stiff peaks. Fold into the lemon mixture until blended. Set aside.

To assemble the Napoléons, set one pastry bottom slice on a tray. Spread with a spoonful of lemon cream and top with a single layer of strawberry slices. Add another pastry layer and repeat. Add a top pastry layer (the more puffed and golden ones). Repeat until all the layers have been used. The numbers won't work so that you always have a bottom pastry layer on the bottom, which is fine, but you do need a top layer on top for aesthetic reasons. Refrigerate until needed (no more than 6–8 hours).

Dust with confectioners' sugar before serving, allowing 1–2 Napoléons each.

light desserts

Poached peaches are a very simple and elegant way to end a heavy meal. To jazz it up a bit, serve the peaches with Raspberry Coulis (page 62) and vanilla ice cream and, *voilà*, Peach Melba, the famous dessert created by Escoffier for the great soprano, Dame Nellie Melba.

poached peaches in vanilla syrup
les pêches pochées au sirop vanillé

½ cup sugar

1 vanilla bean, split

6 peaches, ripe but not too soft

sweetened crème fraîche or whipped cream, to serve

parchment paper

serves 6

Pour 6 cups water into a saucepan. Add the sugar and vanilla bean, bring to a boil, then simmer gently.

Bring another saucepan of water to a boil. Make a criss-cross incision in the base of each peach and plunge it into the boiling water for 30 seconds. Remove with a slotted spoon. Using a small knife, peel off the skin. Transfer the peeled peaches to the sugar syrup as they are peeled. Cover with a round of parchment paper and poach until tender, 15–25 minutes depending on ripeness.

Remove from the syrup with a slotted spoon. Raise the heat under the saucepan and boil the syrup to reduce by half. Let cool.

Serve in small bowls, with some of the poaching liquid and a dollop of the cream of your choice.

This is a classic recipe for poached pears, but you can also poach them in the same way as the peaches (page 11), then serve with a chocolate sauce and vanilla ice cream—also known as *Poires Belle Hélène*.

poached pears in honey wine
les poires pochées au vin et au miel

1 bottle of fruity red wine, 750 ml

½ cup honey

a pinch of ground cinnamon

6 pears, ripe but not too soft

sweetened crème fraîche or whipped cream, to serve

serves 6

Put the wine, honey, and cinnamon in a saucepan large enough to take all the pears snugly in one layer, stems upward. (Don't add the pears yet.) Bring to a boil, then simmer gently.

Using a vegetable peeler, peel the fruit, also leaving the stems intact. Put into the poaching liquid, stems upward. Poach until tender, 15–25 minutes depending on ripeness. Remove from the syrup with a slotted spoon. Raise the heat under the saucepan and boil the honey wine to reduce by half. Let cool.

Serve in small bowls, with some of the honey wine and a dollop of the cream of your choice.

The sweet and frothy egg mixture spread on top of the fruit is called a *sabayon*, making this a very easy and elegant dessert. It is best when made with a bit of something alcoholic—I prefer Muscat de Beaumes de Venise. The recipe requires only a small amount of wine and the remainder is just the thing to drink with this dish—ideal for special occasions.

berry gratin *gratin de fruits des bois*

1¼ lb. frozen mixed berries, (or two 10 oz. packages) thawed

5 extra-large egg yolks and 3 egg whites

⅓ cup sugar

1 tablespoon honey

½ cup sweet dessert wine or champagne (optional)

1–2 tablespoons confectioners' sugar

4 shallow, ovenproof gratin dishes

serves 4

Divide the fruit between the gratin dishes. Preheat the broiler to high.

Bring a saucepan of water just to simmering point. Choose a heatproof bowl (glass is ideal) that will sit tightly on top of the saucepan. Put the egg yolks and sugar in the bowl and whisk, off the heat, until blended. Transfer the bowl to the saucepan and continue whisking, over the heat, until the mixture is thick and frothy, 2–4 minutes. Don't let the water boil. Whisk in the honey and wine or champagne if using, and remove from the heat.

Beat the egg whites in another bowl until they hold stiff peaks.

Gently fold the beaten whites into the warm yolk mixture until blended. Divide between the gratin dishes, spreading evenly to cover the fruit. Lightly sprinkle the top of each with a dusting of confectioners' sugar (this will help it to color nicely). Cook under the hot broiler until just browned, 1–2 minutes (watch carefully because they will color quite quickly). Serve immediately.

Variation Use fresh berries when in season. Raspberries and strawberries are best, mixed or on their own.

This unusual way to make chocolate mousse came from my friend's mother in a letter posted from a village outside Toulouse. It was beautifully hand-written in old-fashioned French schoolgirl script, very neat and curvy. And a good recipe it is too. She uses confectioners' sugar, which makes it smoother, and crème fraîche for a pleasant tang.

chocolate mousse
mousse au chocolat

6 oz. bittersweet chocolate, finely chopped

4 tablespoons unsalted butter

5 extra-large eggs, separated

⅓ cup confectioners' sugar

¼ cup sugar

6 tablespoons crème fraîche or heavy cream

serves 6

Put the chocolate in a microwave-proof bowl and microwave on HIGH for 40 seconds. Remove, stir, and repeat until almost completely melted. Remove and stir in the butter. Set aside.

Put the egg whites and the confectioners' sugar in another bowl and beat until they hold firm peaks. Set aside.

Put the egg yolks and sugar in a third bowl and beat until slightly thickened and a paler yellow. Using a spatula, fold in the cream. Stir in the chocolate mixture.

Add one-third of the beaten whites and mix until no streaks of white remain. Gently fold in the remaining whites, blending well but taking care not to overmix or you will deflate all the whites.

Transfer to individual serving dishes and refrigerate 6–8 hours, or overnight. Serve chilled.

Note If you don't have a microwave, put the chocolate in a bowl over a saucepan of simmering water—don't let the water touch the bottom of the bowl. Leave until melted, stirring occasionally.

This very old-fashioned recipe evokes cries of "*oo-la, les petits pots …*" from French acquaintances of a certain age. It's the sort of thing an auntie would have made in the kitchen of her country house during the summer vacation. And most respectable aunties would have had special little pots, about the size of espresso cups, solely for this purpose. You can also use regular crème brûlée ramekins. Good-quality chocolate is imperative.

chocolate cream pots
petits pots au chocolat

1 cup whole milk

1 cup heavy cream

3½ oz. bittersweet chocolate, finely chopped

3 whole eggs and 2 egg yolks

⅔ cup sugar

6 ramekins or other heatproof containers

a baking dish

serves 6

Put the milk and cream in a saucepan. Bring to a boil and remove from the heat. Stir in the chocolate until melted.

Put the eggs, yolks, and sugar in a large bowl and mix well, but don't whisk until frothy; the finished dish should be smooth on top and whisking too much will make too many bubbles that mar the surface. Pour in the milk mixture and stir gently until just mixed.

Bring a kettle of water to a boil and preheat the oven to 350°F.

Set the ramekins in a baking dish. Ladle the chocolate mixture into each ramekin to fill well. Open the preheated oven, pull out the shelf, and set the baking dish with the ramekins on the shelf. Pour the boiling water into the baking dish to come about two-thirds up the sides of the ramekins. Carefully push the shelf back in.

Cook until just set and still a bit jiggly in the middle, 25–30 minutes. Remove the baking dish from the oven, set aside for 5 minutes, then remove the ramekins from the water bath. Let cool uncovered. Serve warm or at room temperature.

A lot of fuss is made about making soufflés, but it's really not that complicated. The main mixture can be prepared ahead of time, leaving you with nothing more than whisking egg whites and baking just before serving. It will inevitably fall as it cools, or when you stick a spoon in it, but this doesn't affect the taste in the slightest.

vanilla orange soufflé
soufflé au vanille et à l'orange

1 cup whole milk

1 vanilla bean, split

1 tablespoon freshly grated orange zest, from an unwaxed organic orange if possible

4 extra large egg yolks and 6 egg whites

½ cup sugar

3 tablespoons all-purpose flour

1 tablespoon Grand Marnier liqueur (optional)

a deep soufflé dish, about 6½ inches diameter, buttered and dusted with superfine sugar

serves 4

Put the milk and vanilla bean in a saucepan set over medium heat. Bring to a boil, then cover and set aside to infuse for 15 minutes.

Put the orange zest, egg yolks, and all but 1 tablespoon of the sugar in a large bowl and whisk until slightly thickened and a paler yellow. Whisk in the flour and the Grand Marnier, if using.

Scrape the vanilla seeds into the milk, then discard the pod. Gradually whisk the hot milk into the yolk mixture, then return to the saucepan and set over low heat. Cook, stirring constantly with a wooden spoon, until thick enough to coat the back of the spoon, 2–3 minutes. Let cool. (The recipe can be made up to 24 hours in advance to this stage, then cover and refrigerate until needed.)

Preheat the oven to 400°F.

Put the egg whites and remaining sugar in a separate bowl and beat until firm and glossy. Fold one-third of the egg whites into the cooled orange mixture until blended, then carefully but thoroughly fold in the rest.

Transfer to the prepared dish and put in the oven. Lower the heat to 350°F. Bake until puffed and just browned, 20–30 minutes. Serve immediately.

This traditional French dessert is also called *Oeufs à la Neige* (Snow Eggs). Before the advent of the microwave, it involved a very fussy poaching procedure. I would never have bothered to make it at home myself, but cooking the meringues in the microwave makes this super-simple, so it's back on the menu. The custard and egg whites can be made a few hours in advance (keep cool and return to room temperature to serve), but the caramel must be last-minute.

floating islands *îles flottantes*

6 extra-large egg whites

3 tablespoons confectioners' sugar

slivered almonds, to serve

custard sauce

2 cups whole milk (or half milk, half cream)

1 vanilla bean, split

5 extra-large egg yolks

6 tablespoons sugar

caramel

½ cup sugar

a squeeze of lemon juice

6 small microwave-proof ramekins

serves 6

To make the custard sauce, put the milk and vanilla bean in a saucepan and bring just to a boil. Cover and leave to infuse off the heat for 15 minutes.

Put the yolks and sugar in a heatproof bowl and whisk until slightly thickened and a paler yellow. Gradually stir the hot milk into the egg yolk mixture, then return all to the saucepan set over very low heat. Continue stirring until the mixture is thick enough to coat the back of the spoon, 2–3 minutes. Do not let it boil or it will curdle. Remove from the heat and let cool.

Put the egg whites and confectioners' sugar in a bowl and beat until stiff. Divide the whites between 6 ramekins, filling to the top. Put 2 ramekins in the middle of the microwave, so the dishes touch in the middle of the oven. Cook on LOW for 30 seconds. Check, and then repeat for 30 seconds more. The eggs will puff up like a soufflé. If they are not completely firm through, cook for a further 30 seconds. Repeat until all 6 ramekins are cooked. Pry the "islands" gently out of the ramekins—they should slide out with a little prodding.

When ready to serve, put 2–3 spoonfuls of custard sauce in 6 shallow soup plates. Put a poached puffed egg white puff in the middle of each, then prepare the caramel.

Put the sugar, lemon juice, and 3 tablespoons water in a heavy saucepan and cook, stirring, until it turns a light caramel color. Trickle some caramel over each egg white puff and sprinkle with the almonds. Serve at room temperature.

You don't need any special equipment to make a really fantastic frozen dessert, as this recipe will prove. It is also easy, fast, and probably takes first place ahead of all the other recipes in this book. Hard to believe, but this is better than chocolate cake. You can also freeze it in individual silicone molds, but be sure to choose a shape that will allow for a meringue in the middle of each one.

honey parfait with meringue and caramelized pistachios
parfait meringué au miel et aux pistaches caramelisées

1 cup shelled pistachios

¼ cup sugar

1¼ cups heavy cream, chilled

2 eggs, separated

scant ⅓ cup honey

8–10 mini meringues
or 6–8 meringue nests

*a loaf pan or other
freezerproof mold*

serves 6

Put the pistachios and sugar in a nonstick saucepan. Cook over medium-high heat, stirring, until they begin to caramelize. Remove from the pan and let cool. Grind coarsely in a food processor or by putting between 2 sheets of parchment paper and crushing with a rolling pin.

Put the cream in a large bowl and beat until firm. Set aside. Put the egg yolks and honey in a second bowl, whisk well, then set aside. Put the egg whites in a third bowl and beat until they hold stiff peaks. Set aside.

Fold the egg yolk mixture into the cream until blended. Gently fold in the egg whites until just blended. Fold in the pistachios.

Spoon half the mixture into a freezerproof mold (I use a loaf pan because it fits in the freezer more easily and because the mixture seems to freeze more evenly in this shape). Arrange the meringues on top in a single layer—nests may have to be broken up slightly depending on size, but not too small, because you want big pieces of meringue in the finished dish. Cover with the remaining parfait mixture and smooth the top. Cover with plastic wrap and freeze until firm, about 6–8 hours or overnight. Scoop into tall glasses or pretty mugs to serve.

This French café classic is not quite milk shake, not quite sundae, and the result is something that is more grown-up than both, but no less enticing. It is very informal and the ideal thing to serve for a large gathering or an al fresco meal. Use good-quality ice cream for the best result.

ice cream with chocolate sauce and whipped cream
chocolate liegeois

1 cup heavy cream, chilled

2½ cups whole milk

vanilla ice cream

chocolate ice cream

slivered almonds, to serve

chocolate sauce

1 cup sugar

1 cup unsweetened cocoa powder, plus extra for dusting

1 tablespoon instant coffee

serves 4

To make the chocolate sauce, put the sugar and 1½ cups water in a saucepan, stir, bring to a boil, then remove from the heat and stir in the cocoa and coffee. Let cool.

When ready to serve, whip the cream until firm.

Put the milk and the chocolate sauce in a pitcher or bowl and mix until well blended. Divide between 4 tall glasses. Add 1 scoop each of chocolate and vanilla ice cream. Top each with a dollop of whipped cream and dust with cocoa. Sprinkle with the almonds. Serve with long spoons and straws.

In pastry shops, you often see this mousse cake with a thin, shimmering layer of raspberry jelly on top—which you could make if you are so inclined. I find it unnecessary in terms of flavor; fresh raspberries and whipped cream are better, and more than enough ornamentation. A bit of grated chocolate or chocolate curls are good too.

raspberry bavarois *bavarois aux framboises*

1 recipe 3-egg genoise (page 63)

about 12 oz. raspberries, fresh or frozen and thawed, plus 1 small basket of fresh raspberries, to serve

3 sheets of leaf gelatin, or ½ envelope or ½ tablespoon powdered gelatin

custard sauce

2 cups whole milk (or half milk, half cream)

5 egg yolks

6 tablespoons sugar

whipped cream

1 cup heavy cream, chilled

2 tablespoons sugar

a springform cake pan, 9 inches diameter, lined with parchment paper and buttered generously

a pastry bag fitted with a star tip

serves 6

Using a serrated knife, carefully cut the genoise in two, to obtain 2 thin layers. You will need only the bottom one—keep the other for another use.

Put the raspberries in a blender or food processor and blend until smooth, then press through a fine-mesh strainer to obtain a smooth purée; you should have about 1 cup. Set aside.

To make the custard sauce, put the milk in a saucepan and bring just to a boil. Meanwhile, put the yolks and sugar in a heatproof bowl and whisk until slightly thickened and a paler yellow. Gradually stir the hot milk into the egg yolk mixture, then return all to the saucepan set over very low heat. Continue stirring until the mixture is thick enough to coat the back of the spoon, 2–3 minutes. Do not let it boil or it will separate. Remove from the heat and set aside to cool.

When the custard sauce is finger-hot, prepare a bowl of warm (not boiling) water. Dip in the gelatin sheets one at a time to soften, then transfer to the custard and stir well to dissolve each one. Stir in the raspberry purée. If using other forms of gelatin, follow the directions on the package.

Put the thin cake layer into the same springform pan you baked it in, cut side up. Set it on a tray that will fit in your refrigerator (to catch any leaks). Pour the raspberry mixture into the pan and refrigerate until set, 6–8 hours or overnight.

To serve, put the cream and sugar in a bowl and whip until firm. Transfer about one-third into the pastry bag and pipe rosettes around the bottom of the cake. Serve the rest of the whipped cream on the side.

I once stayed with a family in the Provençal village of Crest, where I remember having something similar made with *fraise des bois* (wild strawberries) and then again, with another family in Alsace, made with blueberries we had spent the afternoon gathering. But I also came across a recipe in an Elizabeth David book, which is what reminded me of its existence.

raspberry cream
crème aux framboises

12 oz. raspberries, fresh or frozen and thawed, plus 1 small basket of fresh raspberries

5–6 tablespoons sugar, to taste

1 cup heavy cream, chilled

1 egg white

sprigs of mint, to serve

serves 4

Put the raspberries in a blender or food processor, blend until smooth, then press through a fine-mesh strainer to obtain a smooth purée; you should have about 1 cup. Stir in 4–5 tablespoons of the sugar. Set aside.

Put the cream in a large bowl and beat with an electric mixer until it holds firm peaks. Set aside.

Beat the egg white with 1 tablespoon of the sugar until it holds firm peaks. Fold the beaten egg white and raspberry purée into the cream.

Divide the mixture between 4 serving glasses, filling half-way. Set aside 4 fresh raspberries, then divide the remaining fresh ones between the glasses and top with the remaining raspberry cream.

Decorate the top of each with a fresh raspberry and a mint sprig. Chill for up to 6 hours. Serve cold.

Variation If you are able to get fromage frais, you can use it in place of the whipped cream, or use half whipped cream and half fromage frais. This can also be made with strawberries or mixed berries, though you will have to adjust the sugar content. Sweeten the fruit purée gradually, tasting as you go, until it is to your liking.

Preparation of crème caramel is simple, but there are a few tricks to help you with unmolding. First, don't use ramekins that are too deep (and don't overfill them). Then, leave the ramekins in the bain-marie for at least 15 minutes before removing them. Just before serving, run a knife around the inside edge, hold an upturned plate over the top and flip over to release the custard.

crème caramel

3 cups whole milk

1 vanilla bean, split lengthwise with a small sharp knife

¾ cup plus 2 tablespoons sugar

5 extra-large eggs

salt

8 ramekin dishes

a roasting pan to hold the ramekins

serves 8

Put the milk, vanilla bean, and its seeds in a saucepan over medium heat and bring just to a boil. Immediately remove from the heat, cover, and let stand while you make the caramel.

To make the caramel, put ½ cup of the sugar, a pinch of salt, and ¼ cup water in a small, heavy saucepan, preferably with a pouring lip. Heat until the sugar turns a deep caramel color, then remove from the heat. When it stops sizzling, pour carefully into the ramekins. Take care not to let the caramel come into contact with your skin; it is very hot. Set the ramekins in a roasting pan and add enough boiling water to the pan to come half-way up the sides of the ramekins—this is called a bain-marie. Set aside.

Add the remaining sugar and another pinch of salt to the saucepan of warm milk and stir until dissolved. Remove the vanilla bean.

Put the eggs in another bowl and whisk until smooth. Pour the warm milk into the eggs and stir well. Ladle into the ramekins.

Carefully transfer the roasting pan with the ramekins to a preheated oven at 350°F and bake until the custard has set and a knife inserted into the middle comes out clean, 20–25 minutes. Serve at room temperature either in their ramekins or inverted onto a plate so the caramel forms a pool of sweet sauce.

Traditionally, this is made with cherries that have not been pitted, which helps to keep the juices in when baking, and makes it much easier on the cook. However, it is much easier on the end user if they are out and most good kitchenware stores sell a nifty little pit-removing device to help with the task.

clafoutis

1 cup whole milk

1 cup heavy cream

3 extra-large eggs

¾ cup sugar

⅓ cup all-purpose flour

1 vanilla bean, split (optional)

1 lb. cherries, pitted

confectioners' sugar, to serve

a large baking dish, 10 inches diameter, generously buttered and sprinkled with sugar

serves 6

Put the milk, cream, eggs, and sugar in a bowl and mix until thoroughly blended. Add the flour and beat well. If using a vanilla bean, scrape in the seeds with the tip of a small knife, and stir.

Arrange the cherries in a single layer in the prepared dish. Preheat the oven to 400°F.

Set the dish on the oven rack pulled out half-way, then pour over the batter. Gently push the oven shelf back in and bake until puffed and golden, 35–45 minutes. Just before serving, dust with confectioners' sugar and serve warm or at room temperature.

Possibly the most classic of all French classics, so no cookbook on French desserts would be complete without a recipe. That said, when I lived in France, crêpes were either street food (as in Paris), a cheap meal for students, or something made on Sunday evening as a light meal after the long and laden Sunday lunch. I do not ever remember actually eating them as a "fancy" dessert. Never mind. They are a great culinary contribution and more than worthy of inclusion here.

crêpes

scant 2 cups all-purpose flour
3 extra-large eggs, beaten
2 cups whole milk
2 tablespoons sugar
unsalted butter, for cooking

serves 4–6

Put the flour in a large bowl and make a hollow in the middle. Pour the beaten eggs into the hollow. Using a wooden spoon, gradually beat the eggs into the flour. Stir well because you don't want too many lumps. Pour in the milk slowly, stirring constantly, until completely blended. Stir in the sugar. Let stand for at least 1 hour.

Heat a small, nonstick skillet over medium heat. Add a lump of butter, melt, and swirl to coat. Add a ladle of batter to the pan and swirl to spread thinly but evenly. Cook as for regular pancakes, until browning around the edges and bubbly in the middle, then flip over and cook for a few minutes longer.

As a rule, the first few crêpes are not perfect because it takes a while for the pan to get to just the right temperature, and for the cook to get warmed up. Continue cooking until all the batter has been used, occasionally adding more butter as needed. Serve warm, with the filling of your choice.

Fillings
• The best, in my opinion, is a lump of butter run over the hot crêpe, followed by a sprinkling of sugar, then a generous squeeze of lemon juice. Liqueur is also a nice alternative to the lemon juice—try Grand Marnier.
• Try chocolate sauce, jam, thinly sliced apples sautéed in butter, sweetened chestnut purée and crème fraîche, orange flower or rose water, or honey.
• Ice cream and/or whipped cream, optionally sprinkled with chopped nuts, sliced bananas, and/or strawberries.

An absolute classic, this is a lot easier to make at home than you might think. You should invest in the right pan because an ordinary cake pan or tart pan is not suitable. Once you make and taste this, you will come back to it time and time again, so the investment will be more than worthwhile. Crème fraîche is the authentic accompaniment, but simple heavy cream, whipped cream, or even vanilla ice cream are all perfectly good.

tarte tatin
tarte des demoiselles tatin

1 recipe Sweet Pastry Dough (Pâte Brisée), (page 63)

3½ lb. apples (about 9), such as Golden Delicious

1 stick plus 2 tablespoons unsalted butter

¾ cup sugar

a baking sheet

a tarte tatin pan or other flameproof, round baking dish (lined copper or enameled cast iron)

serves 8

Roll out the dough to a disk the diameter of the pan; turn the pan upside down on the rolled out dough, press down, and trace around the edge with the tip of a knife. Transfer the dough circle to a baking sheet and chill until needed.

Peel, core, and quarter the apples. Set aside.

Put the butter and sugar in the tarte tatin pan and melt over high heat, stirring to blend. Remove from the heat and arrange the apples in the pan in 2 circles. The inner circle should go in the opposite direction from the outer circle.

Return to the heat and cook for 30 minutes. From this point, watch the apples carefully and cook for a further 5–15 minutes, until the liquid thickens and turns a golden caramel color. Remove from the heat and put the disk of dough on top, gently tucking in the edges.

Transfer to a preheated oven and bake at 400°F until browned, 45 minutes to 1 hour. Remove from the oven and let cool slightly. Invert onto a serving plate while still warm (or the caramel will harden, making it too difficult). Serve hot, warm, or at room temperature—the pastry should be on the bottom and the fruit on the top.

tartes

In French pastry shops, this tart is often made in a more orderly fashion, with all the fruit arranged in neat circles. I find it is prettier—and more accessible for the home cook—to use the higgledy-piggledy approach to fruit distribution. Pile it as high as you like, but be warned that it can get a bit messy when serving. This does not in any way affect the taste.

fresh fruit tart
tarte aux fruits frais

1 recipe Pastry Cream
(Crème Pâtissière), (page 62)

1 pre-baked Sweet Pastry
(Pâte Brisée) tart crust,
still in its pan (page 63)

fruit filling

1 small basket blackberries

1 small basket blueberries

1 small basket strawberries

1 peach, thinly sliced

1 nectarine, thinly sliced

2 purple plums, thinly sliced

1 kiwifruit, peeled, halved,
and thinly sliced

about ½ cup apricot jam

serves 8–10

Spread the pastry cream in an even layer in the baked tart crust. Arrange the fruit on top. I start with one kind, using almost all of it, and then go on to another, until I've used all the types. Then I go back and fill in the holes with the remaining pieces.

Melt the jam and 2 tablespoons water in a small saucepan over low heat. Strain to remove all the lumpy bits. Using a pastry brush, carefully but generously dab or brush the jam over the fruit to form a shiny glaze. Let cool. Refrigerate 6–8 hours in advance, but return to almost room temperature to serve.

Variation For a fresh strawberry tart, use 2–3 large baskets of washed and dried strawberries, halved and/or sliced depending on size. Glaze with red currant or cranberry jelly instead of apricot jam—it shouldn't need straining.

Every time I make this, I wonder why I don't make it more often. Daily is obviously out, but I would certainly never tire of it. It can easily be made in advance and it always looks good, so it is the ideal choice for entertaining, either intimate gatherings or large crowds. It has the same almond mixture as the Pine Nut Tart on page 46, which is called *tant-pour-tant* (same-for-same) in French, because the recipe is simply equal weights of all four ingredients: butter, sugar, eggs, and almonds.

pear and almond tart

3–4 ripe pears*

1 pre-baked Sweet Pastry (Pâte Brisée) tart crust, still in its pan (page 63)

almond cream

7 tablespoons unsalted butter, softened

½ cup sugar

2 extra-large eggs

4 oz. blanched almonds, finely ground

2 tablespoons all-purpose flour

serves 6

*If only unripe pears are available, poach for 5 minutes in simmering water with the juice of ½ lemon.

To make the almond cream, put the butter and sugar in a large bowl and beat with an electric mixer until light and fluffy. Add the eggs one at a time, beating well after each addition. Stir in the almonds and flour until just blended. Set aside.

Peel the pears and cut into slices. Set aside.

Spread the almond cream in the tart crust in an even layer. Arrange the pear slices on top.

Bake in a preheated oven at 375°F until puffed and golden, 20–25 minutes. Serve warm.

Note To grind the almonds, put them in a clean coffee grinder and pulse until fine.

Almost any fruit can be used for this recipe, which is Alsatian in origin. Plums are especially nice and any variety will do; it's even nicer if you mix yellow, red, and purple plums. Whatever fruit you choose, the amount does depend on the size, but use the weight as a rough guide and allow a bit more, just in case. Try this with peaches, apricots, nectarines, rhubarb, or apples too.

baked fruit and custard tart
tarte aux fruits alsacienne

1 pre-baked Sweet Pastry (Pâte Brisée) tart crust, still in its pan (page 63) baked in a round or rectangular tart pan

tart filling

1½–2 lb. plums, just ripe but not too soft

2 extra-large eggs

⅓ cup heavy cream

6 tablespoons sugar, plus more for sprinkling

a baking sheet

serves 6

To make the tart filling, cut the plums in fourths and remove the pits. Arrange the plums in the tart shell in 2 circles if using a round tart pan, or in lines if using a rectangular pan. If you are using a round pan, the inner circle should go in the opposite direction from the outer circle.

Put the eggs, cream, and sugar in a large bowl and whisk well.

Set the tart shell carefully on a baking sheet and pour the egg mixture over the fruit, taking care to fill the tart evenly.

Transfer to a preheated oven at 400°F and bake until puffed, just set, and beginning to turn golden brown, 35–45 minutes.

Remove from the oven. Sprinkle generously with sugar and serve warm or at room temperature.

This traditional recipe, on its own, is delicious for afternoon tea. To dress it up for dinner, I've added roasted fruit, made just as you would roast vegetables, but sprinkled with citrus juice, butter, and honey. You can make the tart well in advance (one day is fine) and prepare the fruit before serving, or make it all in advance and simply re-warm the fruit to serve.

1 pre-baked Sweet Pastry (Pâte Brisée) tart crust, still in its pan (page 63)

pine nut tart with roasted fall fruit
tarte aux pignons, fruits d'automne rôtis

pine nut filling

1 stick unsalted butter, at room temperature

scant ⅔ cup sugar

⅔ cup pine nuts

2 extra-large eggs

To make the filling, put the butter, sugar, and pine nuts in a bowl and mix with an electric beater. Add the eggs, one at a time, until completely blended. Transfer the mixture to the tart crust. Sprinkle the pine nuts evenly over the top and bake in a preheated oven at 350°F until puffed and golden, 25–30 minutes. Remove from the oven and let cool.

autumn fruit

2 pears, preferably Comice, not too ripe

2 tart apples

2 large plums

4–6 just-ripe figs

freshly squeezed juice of 1 orange

3 tablespoons unsalted butter

2 tablespoons honey

aluminum foil

serves 4

To roast the fruit, raise the oven temperature to 400°F. Quarter the pears, apples, plums, and figs, discarding the pits and cores. Arrange in a shallow baking dish, sprinkle with orange juice, dot with butter, and trickle honey over the top. Cover with foil and roast for 30 minutes. Remove the foil and roast for 10–15 minutes more. Heat the grill to high and cook the fruit under the grill for 1–2 minutes to brown slightly.

Serve the tart at room temperature, with the warm fruit.

Variation Instead of figs, use more plums, perhaps with a few dried apricots.

I must have made a thousand lemon tarts in my day, but I really struggled to get this good enough to publish. The key lessons learned from my mistakes are these. The oven temperature must not be too high or the mixture will curdle unattractively. You really must fill the tart shell on the pulled-out oven shelf; it should be filled right to the top and no one could possibly transfer from counter to oven without spilling. And try not to do too many other things while baking.

lemon tart

tarte au citron

1 pre-baked Sweet Pastry (Pâte Brisée) tart crust, still in its pan (page 63)

confectioners' sugar, to serve

lemon filling

3 lemons

½ orange

1 cup sugar

3 extra-large eggs and 2 egg yolks

scant 1 cup heavy cream

a baking sheet

serves 8–10

To make the filling, squeeze the juice from the lemons and the ½ orange and strain into a bowl. Preheat the oven to 300°F.

Add the sugar, eggs, and egg yolks to the bowl and whisk just enough to blend in the eggs. Do not whisk too vigorously or the mixture will be too frothy. Stir in the cream.

Put the tart crust on a baking sheet and set this on the oven rack, partially pulled out. Pour the lemon mixture through a strainer into the tart crust and carefully slide the oven shelf back into place. Alternatively, strain the mixture into a pitcher, then pour it into the tart crust before sliding the shelf into the oven. Bake until just set, 20–25 minutes. Let cool.

Dust with confectioners' sugar and serve immediately, at room temperature.

This is as easy as—well, almost. You don't have to make an apple purée to go under the apple slices, but what a difference it makes! It is also easy to make this look good. The secret is thinly sliced apples, packed in as tightly as possible and with some patience when you arrange them. It might look a bit lumpy when raw, but the slices soften in the oven and it always comes out looking better than when it went in.

apple tart
tarte aux pommes

1 pre-baked Sweet Pastry (Pâte Brisée) tart crust, still in its pan (page 63)

apple purée

3 Golden Delicious apples, peeled and chopped

1 vanilla bean, split lengthwise with a small sharp knife

2 tablespoons sugar

½ tablespoon unsalted butter

apple topping

3 Golden Delicious apples, peeled and thinly sliced

¾ tablespoon unsalted butter, melted

1 tablespoon sugar

serves 6

To make the apple purée, put the chopped apples, vanilla bean, sugar, and butter in a saucepan, add ¼ cup water, and cook gently, stirring often until soft, adding more water if necessary, about 10–15 minutes. Use the tip of a small knife to scrape the seeds out of the vanilla bean into the purée, then discard the bean. Transfer the mixture to a food processor, blender, or food mill and purée. Spread the purée evenly in the tart crust.

To make the topping, arrange the apple slices in a circle around the edge; they should be slightly overlapping but not completely squashed together. Repeat for an inner circle, trimming the slices slightly so they fit, and going in the opposite direction from the outer circle. Brush with the melted butter and sprinkle with the sugar.

Bake in a preheated oven at 400°F until just browned and tender, 25–35 minutes. Serve warm or at room temperature.

A very simple and elegant tart recipe. The chestnut flavor is subtle but quite pleasant, and it makes the texture much creamier and smoother. This is easily made in advance and kept in the refrigerator until needed (up to 24 hours), but do not serve it chilled; room temperature is ideal.

chocolate chestnut tart

tarte au chocolat et aux marrons

1 pre-baked Sweet Pastry (Pâte Brisée) tart crust, still in its pan (page 63)

whipped cream or sweetened crème fraîche, to serve

unsweetened cocoa powder, for dusting

chocolate chestnut filling

4 oz. bittersweet chocolate, finely chopped

3 tablespoons unsalted butter

1 extra-large egg, beaten

¾ cup heavy cream

8 oz. (1 cup) canned sweetened chestnut purée

a baking sheet

serves 8–10

To make the filling, put the chocolate in a large microwave-proof bowl and melt in the microwave on HIGH for 30 seconds. Remove, stir, and repeat until almost completely melted. Remove, add the butter, and stir until melted.

Stir in the egg, cream, and chestnut purée and mix just to blend.

Put the tart crust on a baking sheet and set this on the oven rack, partially pulled out. (If you try to fill the crust and then transfer it to the oven, it will surely spill over the edges and burn.) Pour the chocolate mixture into the tart crust and carefully slide the oven shelf back into place. Bake in a preheated oven at 300°F until just set, 20–25 minutes. Let cool to room temperature before serving.

Note If you don't have a microwave, put the chocolate in a bowl over a saucepan of simmering water—don't let the water touch the bottom of the bowl. Leave until melted, stirring occasionally.

I learned to make this when I was an exchange student in France. My French "mother" helped me to prepare it for a party at the end of the school year and I have never forgotten how we did it. What I cannot remember is how I got it to the event, because I know I went on the back of my friend's moped. At the time, this was a far more thrilling part of the foreign experience than learning new recipes. But it did get there, somehow, because I remember the compliments.

strawberry shortcake
gâteau aux fraises et chantilly

1–1¼ lb. strawberries, sliced if large, cut in halves or fourths if small

freshly squeezed juice of ½ lemon

⅓ cup sugar

2 cups heavy cream, chilled

1 recipe 4-egg genoise (page 63)

sugar syrup

3 tablespoons sugar

1 tablespoon brandy

a deep cake pan, 9 inches diameter, lined with parchment paper and buttered generously

a pastry bag with fluted tip

serves 8–10

To prepare the sugar syrup, mix the sugar and 5 tablespoons water in a small saucepan. Bring just to a boil and stir to dissolve the sugar. Remove from the heat and stir in the brandy. Set aside.

Put the strawberries in a bowl and squeeze over a little lemon juice. Add 1 tablespoon sugar and toss to coat. Set aside. To make the chantilly cream, mix the remaining sugar and the cream in a large bowl. Beat until it holds stiff peaks. Set aside.

Put the cooked genoise on a board and, using a serrated knife, trace a circle around the top of the cake, about ¾ inch from the edge. Cut down to about 1 inch from the base; don't cut all the way through. Using the knife or your fingers, scoop out the middle of the cake and discard. Basically, you are making a cake crust—a bit like a tart crust, but thicker.

Set the cake on a serving plate. Using a brush, moisten the bottom of the cake with the sugar syrup. Spread a generous layer of chantilly in the bottom. Add the strawberries, mounding in the middle. Using a flat knife, spread chantilly cream around the sides and over the top edge of the cake. Put the remaining chantilly in a pastry bag and pipe rosettes around the rim. Refrigerate until ready to serve. This is best served on the day it is made.

gâteaux

Walnuts figure prominently in the cuisine of the southwest, though I would say this is a traditional all-over-France sort of dessert. It is formal and elegant, but not too fussy. Just the right thing to finish off a Sunday lunch. It is equally nice with a cup of tea and some friendly afternoon chat. This cake keeps well, too, so you can make it a day in advance.

walnut cake
gâteau aux noix

1 stick plus 6 tablespoons unsalted butter, softened

1 cup sugar

1 vanilla bean (optional), split

4 extra-large eggs

1½ cups all-purpose flour

1 cup walnut halves, ground

walnut halves, to decorate

caramel frosting

½ cup sugar

a squeeze of lemon juice

⅔ cup heavy cream

a cake pan, 9 inches diameter, greased

a baking sheet

serves 6-8

Put the butter and sugar in a large bowl and beat until fluffy. Scrape in the vanilla seeds, if using. Add the eggs one at a time, beating well after each addition. Using a spatula, gently fold in the flour and ground walnuts. Transfer to the prepared cake pan.

Bake in a preheated oven at 400°F until browned and a knife comes out clean when inserted in the middle, 25–35 minutes. Let cool slightly, then unmold while still warm.

To make the caramel frosting, put the sugar, lemon juice, and 3 tablespoons water in a heavy saucepan and cook, stirring, until it turns a light caramel color. Carefully add the cream (it can splatter), stirring until blended.

Put the cake on a rack set over a baking sheet to catch the drips. Pour over the frosting in a thin, even layer. Decorate with walnut halves and leave until the frosting has set, at least 2–3 hours.

Note To grind the walnuts, put them in a clean coffee grinder and pulse until fine.

This is one of a family of meringue cakes—each one takes its name from the flavor of buttercream used to fill it. I find buttercream too heavy and a bit fussy, so have made a less traditional version here with a simple chocolate ganache, topped with whipped cream.

almond meringue and chocolate layer cake
gâteau succès au chocolat

almond meringue rounds

6 extra-large egg whites

¾ cup plus 2 tablespoons sugar

1¼ cups blanched almonds, finely ground (see note page 42)

2 tablespoons cornstarch

chocolate ganache

1⅔ cup heavy cream

11 oz. semisweet chocolate, finely chopped, plus extra to grate on top

topping

1¼ cups heavy cream

2 tablespoons sugar

parchment paper

2 baking sheets

a pastry bag fitted with a wide tip

serves 6–8

Trace 3 circles, 8 inches diameter, onto the parchment paper and mark the center point. Put the marked paper on baking sheets and set aside.

To make the meringues, put the egg whites and 2 tablespoons sugar in a bowl and beat until firm peaks form. Put the remaining sugar, the ground almonds, and cornstarch in another bowl and mix well. Gently fold the dry ingredients into the beaten whites until blended.

Transfer one-third of the meringue into the pastry bag. Starting at the middle of one circle, pipe out a round, in a spiral fashion, until you reach the marked edge. Repeat to make 2 more rounds. Alternatively, spread the meringue inside the traced circles with a long, thin spatula, taking care to spread in an even layer so it cooks evenly. Tidy the edges. Bake in a preheated oven at 250°F for 1½–2 hours until firm and dry. Let cool.

To make the ganache, put the cream in a saucepan and bring just to a boil. Remove from the heat and stir in the chocolate until completely melted. Let cool slightly.

To assemble, put 1 meringue on a serving plate. Top with one-third of the ganache. Put another meringue on top, add another third of the ganache, then top with the remaining meringue and the remaining chocolate ganache. Refrigerate until the chocolate has completely cooled.

Whip the cream and sugar until firm and spread on top of the final chocolate layer. Grate some chocolate over the top and refrigerate until needed, at least 3 hours or up to 24 hours. Serve chilled.

Though this recipe does require several mixing bowls, it is very easy to prepare. The effort will be worth while—these luscious little cakes are gooey and chocolatey and the perfect end to an elegant meal. Serve straight from the ramekins, pass around something creamy to pour or dollop—and enjoy!

chocolate and hazelnut soufflé cakes

gâteaux moelleux au chocolat et aux noisettes

3½ oz. semisweet chocolate, finely chopped

7 tablespoons unsalted butter, cut into pieces

2 tablespoons honey

3 eggs, separated

½ cup sugar

6 tablespoons all-purpose flour

a pinch of salt

⅓ cup whole blanched hazelnuts, finely ground in a clean coffee grinder

whipped cream, heavy cream, or sweetened crème fraîche, to serve

6 ramekins

a baking sheet

serves 6

Put the chocolate in a microwave-proof bowl and melt in the microwave on HIGH for 40 seconds. Remove, stir, and repeat until almost completely melted. Remove and stir in the butter and honey. Set aside.

Put the egg whites and 1 tablespoon of the sugar in another bowl and beat until firm peaks form. Set aside.

Put the the egg yolks and remaining sugar in a third bowl and beat until slightly thickened and a paler yellow. Using a spatula, fold in the flour and salt. Mix in the nuts. Add one-third of the beaten whites and mix until no streaks of white remain.

Gently fold in the remaining whites, blending well, but taking care not to overmix or you will deflate all the whites.

Divide the mixture between the 6 ramekins. Set the ramekins on the baking sheet and transfer to the oven, preheated to 350°F. Bake until just puffed and set, but still jiggly in the middle, 12–15 minutes. Serve warm with the cream.

Note If you don't have a microwave, put the chocolate in a bowl over a saucepan of simmering water—don't let the water touch the bottom of the bowl. Leave until melted, stirring occasionally.

basics

raspberry coulis

12 oz. frozen raspberries, thawed

3–4 tablespoons confectioners' sugar

1 tablespoon fresh lemon juice

makes about 2 cups

Put the raspberries, 3 tablespoons of the sugar, and lemon juice in a small food processor and purée. Press through a fine-mesh strainer to remove the seeds. Taste and add more sugar if necessary.

chocolate sauce

1 cup heavy cream

2 tablespoons light corn syrup

10 oz. bittersweet chocolate, finely chopped

makes about 2¾ cups

Put the cream and corn syrup in a saucepan and bring to a boil. Remove from the heat, add the chocolate, and stir until melted. Let cool.

crème chantilly

¼ cup sugar

1 cup heavy cream, chilled

makes about 1¼ cups

Mix the sugar and cream in a large bowl, then beat until it holds stiff peaks.

pastry cream
crème pâtissière

2 cups whole milk
(or half milk and half cream)

1 vanilla bean, split

5 egg yolks

¼ cup sugar

⅓ cup all-purpose flour

makes about 3½ cups

Put the milk and vanilla bean in a heavy saucepan and bring just to a boil. Remove from the heat, cover, and leave to infuse for 15 minutes.

Put the egg yolks and sugar in a heatproof bowl and whisk well. Add the flour and mix well. Strain the milk into the yolk mixture and whisk until smooth. Return to the saucepan and continue cooking over low heat, stirring constantly for 2 minutes. It will thicken. Transfer to a shallow bowl and let cool. (This can be prepared up to 1 day in advance if covered and refrigerated.)

sweet pastry dough

pâte brisée

1½ cups all-purpose flour, plus extra for rolling

2 teaspoons sugar

7 tablespoons cold unsalted butter, cut into pieces

a pinch of salt

a loose-based tart pan, 11 inches diameter, greased and floured

parchment paper and baking beans or weights

makes one tart crust, 11 inches diameter

Put the flour, sugar, butter, and salt in a food processor and, using the pulse button, process until the butter has broken down (5–10 pulses). Add 3 tablespoons cold water and pulse just until the dough forms coarse crumbs; add 1 more tablespoon if necessary, but don't do more than 10 pulses.

Transfer the dough to a sheet of parchment paper, roll into a ball, and flatten to a disk. Wrap in the parchment and chill for 30–60 minutes.

Roll out the dough on a floured work surface to a disk slightly larger than the tart pan. Carefully transfer the dough to the prepared pan, patching any holes as you go and pressing gently into the sides. To trim the edges, roll a rolling pin over the top, using the edge of the pan as a cutting surface. Tidy up the edges and refrigerate until firm, 30–60 minutes.

Prick the dough all over, then line with parchment paper and baking beans. Bake in a preheated oven at 400°F for 15 minutes, then remove the paper and beans and bake until just golden, 10–15 minutes more. Let the tart crust cool slightly before filling.

genoise

I have used 3-egg and 4-egg genoises in this book. The method is the same.

4-egg genoise

4 extra-large eggs

⅔ cup sugar

1 cup all-purpose flour, sifted

unsalted butter, for preparing the pan

3-egg genoise

3 extra-large eggs

6 tablespoons sugar

⅔ cup all-purpose flour, sifted

unsalted butter, for preparing the pan

a deep cake pan, 9 inches diameter, lined with parchment paper and buttered generously

makes 1 cake, 9 inches diameter

Mix the eggs and sugar in a bowl. Beat with an electric mixer on high until light and at least doubled in volume, 10–15 minutes. Be sure to mix well; the air that you beat in is the only thing that makes the cake rise. Using a spatula or whisk, fold in the flour just until blended.

Transfer to the prepared pan and bake in a preheated oven at 350°F until golden and a skewer inserted in the middle comes out clean, 20–25 minutes. Remove from the oven, unmold after 5 minutes, and let cool on a rack. (This can be made up to 1 day in advance— keep covered and refrigerated.)

index

conversion chart

Weights and measures are rounded up or down slightly to make measuring easier.

Volume equivalents:

American	Metric	Imperial
1 teaspoon	5 ml	
1 tablespoon	15 ml	
¼ cup	60 ml	2 fl.oz.
⅓ cup	75 ml	2½ fl.oz.
½ cup	125 ml	4 fl.oz.
⅔ cup	150 ml	5 fl.oz. (¼ pint)
¾ cup	175 ml	6 fl.oz.
1 cup	250 ml	8 fl.oz.

Weight equivalents:

Imperial	Metric
1 oz.	25 g
2 oz.	50 g
3 oz.	75 g
4 oz.	125 g
5 oz.	150 g
6 oz.	175 g
7 oz.	200 g
8 oz. (½ lb.)	250 g
9 oz.	275 g
10 oz.	300 g
11 oz.	325 g
12 oz.	375 g
13 oz.	400 g
14 oz.	425 g
15 oz.	475 g
16 oz. (1 lb.)	500 g
2 lb.	1 kg

Measurements:

Inches	cm
¼ inch	5 mm
½ inch	1 cm
¾ inch	1.5 cm
1 inch	2.5 cm
2 inches	5 cm
3 inches	7 cm
4 inches	10 cm
5 inches	12 cm
6 inches	15 cm
7 inches	18 cm
8 inches	20 cm
9 inches	23 cm
10 inches	25 cm
11 inches	28 cm
12 inches	30 cm

Oven temperatures:

110°C	(225°F)	Gas ¼
120°C	(250°F)	Gas ½
140°C	(275°F)	Gas 1
150°C	(300°F)	Gas 2
160°C	(325°F)	Gas 3
180°C	(350°F)	Gas 4
190°C	(375°F)	Gas 5
200°C	(400°F)	Gas 6
220°C	(425°F)	Gas 7
230°C	(450°F)	Gas 8
240°C	(475°F)	Gas 9